DARE TO BE DULL

I found this at the Omaha airport. I thinks its a survival manual for our state.

DARE TO BE DULL

by Joseph L. Troise

Photographs by Ben Asen
Illustrations by Phil Frank
and Whitney Cookman

BANTAM BOOKS

Toronto • New York • London • Sydney

DARE TO BE DULL
A Bantam Book / October 1983

ISBN 0-553-34046-8

Published simultaneously in the United States and Canada

Bantam Books are published by Bantam Books, Inc. Its trademark, consisting of the words "Bantam Books" and the portrayal of a rooster, is Registered in the United States Patent and Trademark Office and in other countries. Marca Registrada. Bantam Books, Inc., 666 Fifth Avenue, New York, New York 10103.

PRINTED IN THE UNITED STATES OF AMERICA

CW   0   9   8   7   6   5   4   3   2   1

dull /dul'/ [from ME, *dul*; akin to OE *dol,* slow out of the gate, and Latin *dullum,* your uncle Fred] *adj* **1** uncharismatic: NOT TRENDY **2** lacking zip: SLUGGISH **3** habitual: PRE-DICTABLE **4** slightly behind the times: OUT OF IT **5** not adventuresome: PRACTICAL **6** not sparkling: AVERAGE **7** lime-Jell-O-ish: TUNA CASSEROLE-LIKE

ACKNOWLEDGMENTS

The author wishes to thank all of his dear friends for their suggestions and encouragement, without which this book would have undoubtedly been far more exciting. I am especially grateful to all the True Believers: Bill "Wiz" Glanting, Alvin Stilman, Cort Strandberg, John Wolff, Tom Lyon, Joann Hay, Herb & Helen Zisser, Lois Babler (Museum of the Ordinary), Andy Stone, Candi Harper, J. D. Stewart, Becky Wilson (Dull Cuisine), Peter Moore (TV & Cinema), the illustrious illustrator, Phil Frank, Bill Schmidt (*The New York Times*), Victor Zonana (*Wall Street Journal*), UPI, Leif Steinert (Dull Arts), the BBC, the CBC, Timothy Price (CBS News), Rubert Johnson (our English cousin), Ruth Williamson, Winston Smith, Howard Aiken, Marcia Rosser, Ben Asen, Lou Aronica (Bantam Books), Arthur and Richard Pine (my agents) and, last but far from least, the original members of the Dull Men's Club, 1980–1983.

CONTENTS

*A Special Message from the Dull Men's
Advisory Council, Washington, D.C.*

The Dull Finally . . . uh . . . Speak Up

It is hard to believe that only four years ago the Dull Movement in America was but a dream. It is difficult to conceive of how it was then, our beloved country overrun by the menacing forces of trendiness, whose sole purpose was (and still is) to oppress the dull and the near-dull with gold neckchains and white wine, BMWs and designer luggage, arduous sports and expensive adventures, lean cuisine and tight overpriced clothes with other people's names on them.

In the late 1970s, the casualties were many. Afraid and defenseless, we hardly protested the brutalities of fad and fashion. We turned in our domestic station wagons for nasty little french-poodle cars that wouldn't start in winter and could barely hold one case of generic beer; our lovers became our "roommates" and our marriages became "relationships"; we jogged (Oh, god, how we jogged!) and we dressed for success. *Nostra Culpa.* We did everything we were supposed to, everything *except* stand up to the relentless peer pressure that turned good, solid dull citizens into insufferable attention-getters.

Now, of course, things are different. We are strong. We are united. We snap our fingers in contempt at men's bikini underwear and bizarre health foods that taste lousy. Day after day, more and more men all over America . . . nay, all over the world . . . are *Daring to be Dull!* It is not publicity they seek, nor power; rather it is the right to proclaim that they are dull. It is the inalienable right of all people to be *Out of It and Proud of It!*

Only now, as we begin once again to feel dull pride, as we dust off our bowling balls and our golf clubs, our scrabble boards, our crossword puzzles and our Don Ho records, only now does it become clear that our true cultural heroes are those who did *not* compromise in those Dark Times, who never gave an inch when threatened with ostracism and ridicule.

THEREFORE, to the dentists who drilled our teeth, promptly and courteously; to the taxi drivers who took a year to earn what the flashy rock star or hip Hollywood director made in a day; to the postal employees who so faithfully crushed our packages; to the accountants whose quiet dedication and diligence kept our books in good order; to the countless business executives who chose to eat lime Jell-O and tuna fish for lunch; to the millions of office workers who caught the same bus or train at the same time each day; to the skinny or chubby kids with glasses who didn't march in step with their trendy little peers; to William Bendix and Jackie Gleason and Broderick Crawford and Art Carney; to everyone who spent their lives just being themselves . . . it is to *them* that we enthusiastically (if you'll pardon the expression) dedicate this book.

PART ONE

THE FAMOUS SCHOOL FOR DULL MEN HOME STUDY COURSE

CHAPTER ONE

THE FAMOUS SCHOOL FOR DULL MEN

HOME STUDY COURSE AND WHAT IT CAN DO FOR YOU

Some testimonials for
The Famous School for Dull Men
Home Study Course

"Thanks to your efforts we dull people can now come out of the closet and take an honorable place in society."

MR. C. E.
DALLAS, TX

"I have always been dull, without knowing it. You've opened my eyes. Now that I know, I can start *really working on it.*
P.S. I order steak at seafood restaurants."

MR. H. J.
REDONDO BEACH, CA

"I'm now in the banking business, and even though others find it dull, I find it rather exciting. I especially like to walk across the marble floor in our bank lobby and listen to the clicking of the little cleats on the heels of my cordovans."

ANONYMOUS

When you first came in contact with this book, or when you first received it from a caring loved one, it is likely that you took hold of it with trembling hand. Such an emotional reaction is not unusual, not even for the dull or the would-be dull, because this book contains a great power . . . the power to release a person, now and forever, from the pressure, the compulsion, the *addiction* of being hip, with-it, interesting, fascinating, sparkling, brilliant, witty, multifaceted, renaissance, *au courant, de rigueur,* and *cul-de-sac.*

Thousands of our graduates have, upon completion

4

A graduate of *The Famous School for Dull Men* Home Study Course receives his diploma from Founder Joseph Troise. This could be you!

of this Home Study Course, gone on to happier, healthier lives, achieving success without charisma, accomplishment without arrogance, and respect without a public relations agent. The *Famous School for Dull Men* Board of Trustees includes such "Mr. Excitements" as Perry Como, Robert Young, Bruce Jenner, Dr. Joyce Brothers, Marie Osmond, Walter Mondale, John Glenn, Ed McMahon and, if he's still living (we hope so), Don Ho. Someday *your* name might be right up there on our letterhead as well.

But for now, let us proceed one step at a time. As you read this book for the first time, you are at a crossroads in your life. To the left, the tragedy of trendiness. To the right, the abyss of overawareness. The choice is obvious. Let's just hang out right here and relax. No sense looking for trouble, we always say.

A word of caution here! Just because everyone calls

5

you a "real dull guy," and just because you got fifteen copies of this book as a gift, *this does not mean* you have nothing to learn from the Home Study Course. Many a dull man such as yourself, after reading a copy of *Dress for Success,* or *Go For It* or *Looking Out for Number One* in some dark corner of a disreputable bookstore, has run out and dyed his hair, bought a red sports car (or worse, a red sport *coat!*) and plastered his body with designer labels from head to toe. *L.A. Disease* (terminal, chronic, incurable trendiness) can strike *anywhere, anytime.*

We would also like to emphasize that one does not have to be *middle-aged* to take this course and succeed. If Andy Williams and suburban living are not your thing, we can always get you into Barry Manilow and video games. One is never too young to start being dull. Even ten-year-old children can embrace computers and stamp collecting with no trouble whatsoever.

No doubt some of you out there are still apprehensive. You've jogged and mountain-climbed all these years; you drive a Porsche, read *Harper's,* and play backgammon regularly; your lapels are wide and you eat avocado and beansprouts for lunch; you have seven painfully beautiful girlfriends and you fly to Mexico every winter. This is all well and good, we suppose, but let us ask you this: are you *happy*? We mean *really happy*? Do you realize what jogging can do to your knees? Have you heard about what happened to those people on Mt. McKinley last year? And when that Porsche engine blows up (they always do, sooner or later) can you imagine what Hans is going to charge you? And *beansprouts*! You mean to tell us that mankind has struggled from a cave-dwelling existence through the eons of time so that he could eat *beansprouts*? And herpes. What about *herpes*? And you seriously think that the Mexican people like all those stupid gringos messing up their country? Would *you*? Perhaps you have a lot more to mull over than you first supposed. We should think so.

You will notice that the back of this book contains a small wallet-size Graduation Certificate signifying that you have successfully completed this course and have earned the title of Certified Dull Person. Not only does this place you in the ranks of a very select fraternity of dull people, but it also allows you to be uninteresting *whenever* and *wherever* you please. Should you ever find yourself badgered at social functions by hip, trendy people, merely present the card and return to your rations of beer and Fritos. Keep in mind, however, that you should complete the course before removing the card and signing your name to it. Impersonating a dull person is not only cruel and immoral, but it can seriously damage any further possibility of rehabilitation on your part. Remember, dullness is *not* just another trend; it is a Way of Life.

CHAPTER TWO

PRELIMINARY TESTING

How Dull Are You Anyway, Huh?

Testing your Dullness Quotient is simple and painless. Don't expect to be perfect. You've got to remember that you've been under pressure to be trendy ever since you were a child.

Answer each question carefully. Then total up your score and compare it to the test results at the end of the examination. Armed with this new self-knowledge—about where you are strong and where you need help—you can then lead yourself to the sublime Sanity of Dullness, which has brought so much joy to so many formerly troubled people.

▬ Testing Your Dullness Quotient ▬

Directions: Answer either *yes* or *no* for each question. Take your time, but stay awake.

1. Do you dress in such a way as to often be mistaken for an off-duty cop?

2. When you jog, does your cigar keep going out?

3. Do you drive a domestic automobile? (You get twice as many points if you have four doors.)

4. Have you ever been kicked out of a public library for being too quiet?

5. When you go to a restaurant, do you usually order meat loaf or chicken salad?

6. Do you think E.R.A. stands for Earned Run Average?

7. Do you think est means Eastern Standard Time?

8. Are you now or have you ever been a Shriner, Rotarian, Elk, Odd Fellow, or Kiwani?

Welcome Wagon count?

9. Were you *very* upset about 1982's NFL strike?

10. Do you think Walter Mondale is a "pretty funny guy?"

11. Do you own a dog named Queenie, Blackie, Brownie, or Fluffy?

12. Do you refer to the woman you live with as your "wife?"

13. Do you address female adults as Miss or Mrs.?

*Von
Please note↑*
14. Do you think exerting yourself is something you should do only when someone is chasing you?

15. As a child, did you ever want to be a dentist?

16. Does Dr. Joyce Brothers "turn you on?"

17. Are your t-shirts plain white with nothing written on them? *I have one that says Amity vineyards from Oregon.*

18. Do you like to alphabetize things?

19. Do you like lime Jell-O?

20. Is there a pair of corduroy slippers in your closet?

21. Do you enjoy listening to freeway traffic reports?

22. Do you know where the Bowling Hall of Fame is located? (Score double if you've actually *been* there.)

23. Do you drink Manhattans?

24. Do you know lots of ethnic jokes, knock-knock jokes or "How many . . ." jokes?

25. Have you ever framed a Norman Rockwell print?

▬▬▬ Test Results ▬▬▬

Scoring: Give yourself 4 points for each *yes* answer, zero for each *no* answer.

Score of 84–100: Hey, hey! Do we have talent here or what? After you've finished the course work (merely perfunctory in your case), give us a call. We're looking for instructors.

Score of 68–80: Not bad, not bad. This is a very respectable score for a first-time tester. You are accepted as a candidate for the Home Study Course. Congratulations!

Score of 62: This isn't really much to brag about, but on the other hand we should consider that you can't get a score of 62 unless you add wrong, which means there may be some hidden talent here. We'd like you to try the Home Study Course. What the hell. Even Harvard takes a couple of weirdos every term, right?

Score below 64: We know what you're thinking. You're a failure. A fraud. Torn between the dull and the trendy. Well, we've decided that no man with the desire to be dull shall be denied the opportunity. Would you like to try a few chapters of the Home Study Course? Good, good.

PART TWO

THE DULL WAY OF DOING THINGS

CHAPTER THREE

THE JOYS OF DULL LIVING

The Dull Way means following the path of living with things you find comfortable and reassuring. Surely no two objects tend to reinforce one's statement about life and how to live it better than a) your house, and b) your car.

Study the following diagrams carefully and notice how both car and home reflect a tasteful yet practical dullness. Of course, our prescriptions are not carved in concrete. Many variations in dull living are possible, and you will no doubt begin to come up with ideas of your own, such as aluminum lawn furniture, smile stickers, and membership in the A.A.A.

After you have given careful attention to both the residence and automotive visuals, proceed to the Review Exercises. Go to the bathroom before you start, and set your Timex digital watch so that it beeps in one-half hour.

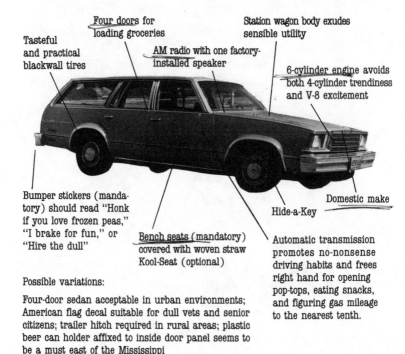

Four doors for loading groceries

Station wagon body exudes sensible utility

Tasteful and practical blackwall tires

AM radio with one factory-installed speaker

6-cylinder engine avoids both 4-cylinder trendiness and V-8 excitement

Bumper stickers (mandatory) should read "Honk if you love frozen peas," "I brake for fun," or "Hire the dull"

Bench seats (mandatory) covered with woven straw Kool-Seat (optional)

Domestic make

Hide-a-Key

Automatic transmission promotes no-nonsense driving habits and frees right hand for opening pop-tops, eating snacks, and figuring gas mileage to the nearest tenth.

Possible variations:

Four-door sedan acceptable in urban environments; American flag decal suitable for dull vets and senior citizens; trailer hitch required in rural areas; plastic beer can holder affixed to inside door panel seems to be a must east of the Mississippi

The Dull Car

I must get a bumper sticker!

Absence of sun decks prevents noisy outdoor parties and frivolous sun-bathing

Large roof perfect for installation of massive satellite TV dish

Apartment units are absolutely identical, encouraging non-competitive attitudes and a sense of equality

Convenient basement snack and cigarette machines make going outside rarely necessary

Steep stairs discourage visitors, salesmen and religious fanatics

Tasteful beige and brown exterior compliments the common-sense institutional architecture

The Dull Apartment

Small garden provides shelter and <u>balanced diet for indigenous</u> <u>animals and insects</u>

North Platte house

Practical metal windows set off by lovely non-operable shutters

Entire side of house serves as garage and laundry room

Imitation chimney for imitation fireplace

Low-maintenance aluminum siding

Electric or gas-fired barbeque

Imitation <u>brick veneer</u> adds that "quality look"

Front lawn serves as putting green or for weekend fun with garden tools

<u>Suburban location offers</u> easy access to Sears stores

Possible variations:

Small grotto (Italian families only); flag pole (VFW members only)

The Dull Home

Review Exercises for Chapter Three
(65% or better is passing)

1. List, in order of preference, the cities you would like to live in.

Albany, New York   _____
Los Angeles, California   _____
Rifle, Colorado   _____
Pisgah, Iowa   _____
Boston, Massachusetts   _____
Bangor, Maine   _____

Vernon, Florida	_____
Sausalito, California	_____
Labette, Kansas	_____
Roachdale, Indiana	_____

Any arrangement is correct as long as you put Los Angeles at the bottom (score 100%). If Los Angeles appeared in the bottom five, this is partially correct (65%). If you left Los Angeles *out,* score double (200%).

I got 200%

2. Here's a reprint of a quiz from *Careful Driver* magazine. Choose either *a, b,* or *c* for each question.

If you won a Lamborghini in a contest, would you:
   a) Show it to all your friends.
   b) Sell it and buy a mobile home.
   c) If I won a *what?*

The speed limit on our nation's highways should be:
   a) no limit whatsoever.
   b) 55 mph.
   c) 55 mph for American cars, 35 mph for foreign cars.

The most important piece of equipment on any car is:
   a) a sunroof.
   b) a 40-channel CB radio.
   c) a completely equipped first aid kit.

When visiting a National Park by automobile, you should:
   a) Park your car in a designated area so as to protect the local ecology.
   b) Locate your car near park facilities.
   c) Choose high ground for good TV reception.

Answer: Score 25 for each *c* answer, 20 for each *b*, zero for each *a*

Final Totals

Your total for question #1 _____

Added to total for #2 _____

Less deductions from line 64, page
5, form 1041B (disregard if
irrelevant) _____

Your combined score for two
questions _____

Divided by two (round to nearest
tenth) _____

Your final total real actual score _____

NOTE: If you fail to achieve a score of 65% on this test please take the following Make-Up Question:

Official Make-Up Question

You're walking along a lonely stretch of beach. Suddenly, you notice an ancient-looking oil lamp sticking out of the sand. You pick it up and begin rubbing it to clean it off. POOF! An immense genie appears, and tells you he will grant you three wishes. What do you do?

a) I wish for youth, money and power.
b) I wish for a cold six-pack, some chrome wheels for my pickup, and a date with Donna Fargo.
c) Sorry, I don't talk to strangers.

Answer: Choosing *c* is worth 100%, *b* is worth 65%, *a* is worth zero.

CHAPTER FOUR

THE UNDERWHELMING WARDROBE

Dull men believe in Goodwill. In fact, they look like they shop there all the time. One's wardrobe is a personal statement to the world, and it is self-defeating, if not downright harmful, for a man's clothes to be in conflict with his true personality. Let's take a look at the kind of inconspicuous elegance that can be achieved, whether at work or play, by avoiding the trendy and transitory. You, as the Total Dull Person, are not dressing for success, to impress, or to excess. You're dressing the same way you did ten years ago.

The Absolute "Musts"

Dark, solid suits, preferably of synthetic fiber, with narrow lapels, belt loops, and cuffs. The cut should be full, especially at the waist and thighs. Sleeves should fall slightly short of the fingernails.

Plain white dress shirts, with insertable plastic tabs for the collar (use optional). Cufflinks with a corporate or fraternal logo are highly recommended. *Casual shirts* can be short-sleeved polyester in either a plain weave or knit, or for cooler weather, long-sleeved flannels will keep you out of the swing of things.

Footwear should consist of stretchable executive *socks* in brown, black, grey, and dark blues and greens. White athletic socks add a touch of manliness, but top stripes should be avoided. *Shoes* should be either a black or brown lace-up or a loafer with tassles. For around the house, corduroy or sheepskin bedroom slippers are the perfect touch.

Appropriate headgear includes grey or brown fedoras, à la Karl Malden; for everyday use, an adjustable mesh cap (with a beer or truck logo) works nicely, and for the dull sportsman a white or light blue "skipper's" cap will keep the sun off that bald spot. For colder climes, a green or red flannel plaid cap with pull-down ear flaps will serve to accent your three-quarter-length *casual jacket* of either shiny vinyl, simulated wool weave, or flannel to match your cap. Large wooden buttons complete the ensemble. During the first hint of autumn, those of you in the temperate zones might prefer a *Perry Como* sweater-vest to the heavier materials. This type of "professorial" wardrobe is nicely accented by a belt-loop pipe holder.

Casual slacks, such as chinos or polyester knits, are appropriate. *Jeans* are generally déclassé for the dull man, unless they are an obscure off-brand made in Poland or Hong Kong for a large discount chain store.

Underwear for the dull man should be practical white boxer shorts and t-shirts, although some "spice" might be added by not immediately mending a few seam rips.

For those *miscellaneous accoutrements,* no underwhelming wardrobe is complete without monogrammed white handkerchiefs, a plastic pocket liner for ball point pens, a few narrow ties (and a tie clip, of course!), a pair of full-cut bermuda shorts, and last but not least, your favorite black high-top sneakers.

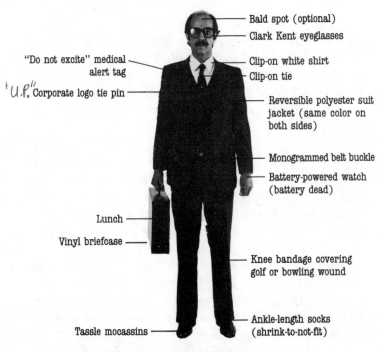

Bald spot (optional)

Clark Kent eyeglasses

"Do not excite" medical alert tag

"U.P." Corporate logo tie pin

Clip-on white shirt

Clip-on tie

Reversible polyester suit jacket (same color on both sides)

Monogrammed belt buckle

Battery-powered watch (battery dead)

Lunch

Vinyl briefcase

Knee bandage covering golf or bowling wound

Ankle-length socks (shrink-to-not-fit)

Tassle mocassins

The Properly Attired Dull Man

━━━━━ Dull Man's Quiz #1 ━━━━━

Q. How can you recognize a dull man's motorcycle?

A. It's the one with the trainer wheels.

34

CHAPTER FIVE

THE JOY OF DULL SEX

Dull men need love, too. Unfortunately, the search for the affections of a good dull woman is fraught with danger. Sometimes the drive for love and comfort from the opposite sex compels perfectly normal, decent dull guys to pretend they are suave, sexy, and excruciatingly cute. This rarely works.

This chapter is designed to help you find a dull soul-mate in a dignified human way, without need of trendy claptrap and dreadful fern bars. Make careful note of the suggestions offered, then go on to the test questions.

Helpful Hints for Dull Singles #1: The Personals Ad

Never underestimate the power of advertising. Sometimes a simple ad that describes who you are and what you're looking for in a woman is the best way to land a date with a dull Miss.

Here's an example of the kind of ad that has worked for quite a few dull guys. If you have some difficulty with the abbreviations, consult the Glossary of Terms.

D/M, fortyish, gets tired quickly, sub., into B&D, seeks dom., bi. U/F into S&M. No pros. Call Ralph before 8:30 PM. 555-1199.

GLOSSARY OF TERMS	
D/M	Dull male
sub.	substitute teacher
B&D	bowling and drinking
dom.	domesticated
bi.	bifocaled
U/F	uninteresting female
S&M	sewing and macrame
No pros	no prospects

Helpful Hints for Dull Singles #2:
A Perfect Date

If you don't have the time to join *Club Dead* (see Chapter Seven), you can still avoid a trendy and painfully self-conscious social life by following these guidelines for a nice, dull dating experience.

The First Date:

5:30 P.M. Meet your date after work for dinner at Taco John's, the Midway Diner, Leon's Bar-B-Que or Wendy's.

6:15 P.M. Walk to movie or take a bus. If you must drive, finish your dinner quickly so that you'll have plenty of time to find a parking place. Movies at the Public Library are best, but a "G" rated movie at a shopping center cinema is acceptable.

7:45 P.M. Go for a nightcap (beer is best) at Walter's Tavern or similar type of bar where people under forty are viewed with suspicion. Play one or two games of either shuffleboard or bumper pool, but not both.

8:30 P.M. After a few beers, spend a *minimum* of fifteen minutes deciding what to do next. It's best to agree on something and then change your mind again. Not only does this consume time, but it tends to discourage spontaneity.

9:00 P.M. After the conversation falls silent and no new plans come to mind, decide to go home. This can be initiated by making stretching gestures and then standing up. The man should always go back to the woman's home or apartment. Holding hands is permissible at this point, unless palms start to sweat.

9:15 P.M.	If you are invited in for tea or coffee, talk about boot camp, your job, or where you used to live before moving to your present residence.
9:30 P.M.	Begin to make stretching gestures again, along with squinting expressions while looking at your watch or a wall clock. Say something to help bring the evening to a close, like "Well, I'd better turn in. I've got to get to the bank pretty darn early tomorrow." Your date will appreciate this. If she walks you to the door, shake her hand goodnight and promise to see her again. Do not, however, specify when.

The Second Date and Beyond:

As above, spacing out dates to once a week. After the third date, begin kissing, but only after excusing yourself to brush your teeth. Continue this schedule for two years, then get engaged. One year after that, get married, then review the *Dull Living* section of this book.

Helpful Hints for Dull Singles #3: The Dull Women's Auxilliary

Ah, the Dull Woman! Somewhat inconspicuous among her more fashionable sisters, this rhinestone in the rough must often be searched for lovingly and skillfully. Indeed, the Women's Auxilliary of the International Dull Men's Club was formed with an eye on bringing these women together under the unity of Dull Pride—allowing them to exercise their right to dress out of fashion, to ignore excruciating weight-loss diets, and to avoid sparkling conversation.

But still, being naturally a bit shy, many Dull Women have yet to become card-carrying members of the Auxilliary. Therefore, we provide the following guide to spotting that wallflower waiting to bloom, that watermelon ready to pick from the vine.

The Dull Man and Woman on a Date

How to Spot the Dull Woman

At a Party:
The one in the corner knitting a little cardigan for her niece.

At an Office Party:
The one who brought her work.

At the Beach:
The one wearing the one-piece bathing suit with ruffled skirt.

At a Dance:
The one doing the bunny-hop.

At an Automotive Repair Shop:
The one who has the Volkswagon named "Olivia."

At the Veterinarian:
The one talking baby-talk to her Pekingese (or her parakeet named "pretty boy").

At a Bar:
The one who empties her purse to reveal a wallet photo of Rick Nelson, a plastic rain bonnet, and a date book with a fuzzy picture of two kittens on the cover.

On a First Date:
The one with the small poster taped to her refrigerator which reads "Today is the first day of the rest of your life," next to which is a Weight-Watcher's calorie chart fastened by four magnetic smile buttons.

On a Blind Date:
The one standing under the clock wearing the sugar-cube corsage.

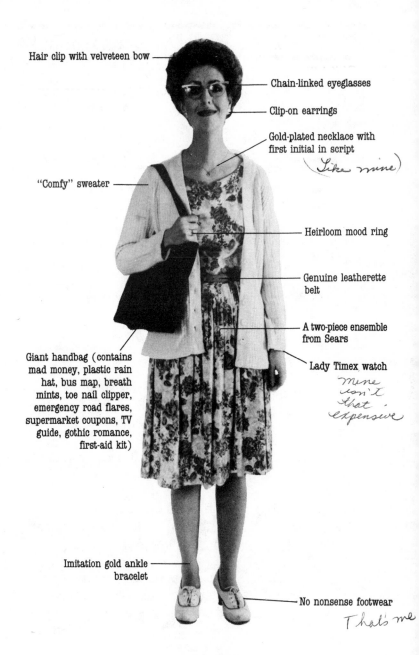

Hair clip with velveteen bow

Chain-linked eyeglasses

Clip-on earrings

Gold-plated necklace with
first initial in script

(like mine)

"Comfy" sweater

Heirloom mood ring

Genuine leatherette
belt

A two-piece ensemble
from Sears

Giant handbag (contains
mad money, plastic rain
hat, bus map, breath
mints, toe nail clipper,
emergency road flares,
supermarket coupons, TV
guide, gothic romance,
first-aid kit)

Lady Timex watch

mine isn't that expensive

Imitation gold ankle
bracelet

No nonsense footwear

That's me

The Dull Date

31

The Dull Man's Wallet-Size Sex Manual

Who knows when love will walk through your aluminum screen door? Keep this page with you at all times, you dull devil!

Great Opening Lines:

"I noticed you weren't dancing. Did you hurt yourself or something?"

"Excuse me, miss. I can't finish this slice of pizza. Would you like the rest of it?"

"I was wondering. Is that a beauty mark or a wart?"

A Brief Explanation of Sexual Terminology

Climax	This is a bit difficult to explain, but think back to the last time your toes curled up.
Deviant Behavior (Perversion)	Making sexual advances before the *Tonight Show*.
Foreplay	Turning off the lights and switching on the AM clock radio. (Variation: "Hey, you awake?")
French Kiss	Usually performed by two consenting French politicians, one of whom is always giving the other a medal at the time. Why *anyone* finds this exciting, we really don't know.

Kinky	More than once a week.
Ménage à Trois	A small french pastry; also, a group of dull people.
Oral Sex	Making love by telephone. This technique is very convenient for people who travel. Calling collect is considered bad form.
Orgasm	This is when the woman makes strange noises. Do not be alarmed. This kind of thing happens once in a while.
Spanish Cartwheel	Not recommended for dull men, although we would be interested in knowing who exactly suggested this to you.

═══════ Après Sex Activities: ═══════

1. Offer your lover some Hawaiian Punch.
2. *Do not* immediately roll over and go to sleep. Count to ten first.
3. Take off your clothes.
4. Tell her you're sorry about the cat.
5. Unlock the bedroom door.

Review Exercises for Chapter Five
(65% is a passing grade)

1. Multiple choice. Select either *a, b,* or *c* for each question:

   If a dull man is going out for a big night on the town, the proper gift for his date would be:

   a) one dozen red roses.

   b) a black and white TV.

   c) a potted geranium.

   Pretend it's your anniversary. A nice present for your wife would be:

   Tom's choices

   a) a bottle of fine perfume.

   b) a blood pressure tester.

   c) a trash compactor.

   For the daring dull guy, a suitable gift for his mistress at Christmas might be:

   a) a diamond brooch.

   b) an Andy Williams record.

   c) snow tires.

   On Mother's Day, the dear woman who brought you into the world would probably love:

   a) a trip to the Caribbean.

   b) a subscription to *National Geographic*.

   c) a gift certificate to the Cheese-of-the-Month Club.

Suggestive and erotic gifts can add a little spice to the dull man's amours. What would you send to that "special someone"?

a) a sheer, scanty negligee.

b) baby-doll pajamas with lots of little hearts sewn on them.

c) see-through ear muffs.

Answers: Score 20 points for each *c* answer; 13 points for each *b* answer; zero points for each *a* answer.

Your final score for this chapter   _____

Note: Should you fail to receive a passing grade of 65% for this chapter, you may then take the make-up question which follows:

▬▬ Official Make-Up Question ▬▬

Picture yourself in the following situation: You stop at your favorite tavern for a drink after work. While you're watching a rerun of *Gilligan's Island* a stunning blonde comes up behind you and whispers in your ear that you are the most fascinating, sexy man she has ever met and could she come home with you? An appropriate reply would be:

a) "Hey, baby, you bet!"

b) "O.K., but could we wait until this show is over?"

c) "I'll have to ask my wife first."

Answer: If you chose *c*, give yourself 100%; for *b*, score 65%; for *a*, zero.

CHAPTER SIX

THE *LOQUI* (lo 'kee) SEARCH FOR SELF-KNOWLEDGE

When Trendiness Strikes ...

... Help Is Near.

Dullwood

A Rehabilitation Center for the Chronically Trendy

It comes without warning, like a thief in the night; it afflicts both rich and poor; it knows neither race nor creed nor social standing. No one is immune when the spectre of trendiness rears its stylish head.

The first signs of trouble are, unfortunately, all too subtle. It may be nothing more than finding a gold neckchain in the corner of a loved one's drawer, next to his socks. It might be only a bottle cap from an imported beer, lying on the floor of the family car; perhaps it is just a passing remark about how the old station wagon doesn't "handle" well and seems "ordinary;" maybe it's nothing more than a casual comment to a waitress about the possibility of getting some beansprouts for that BLT. Yes, the symptoms appear to be so very unimportant in the beginning; yet they will prove to be the prelude to disaster.

The causes of trendiness are still not completely understood. We suspect that advertising, peer pressure and Southern California play a large part, and there is evidence, although sketchy, that some form of genetic transmission is possible. What we *do* know is that trendiness is curable, *if treated in time*.

The highly trained staff of *Dullwood*, under the direction of Swiss physician Dr. Ignatius B. Bland are themselves formerly hip, with-it, multifaceted, sparkling, witty, interesting people who have been successfully rehabilitated. *Dullwood's* staff *has been there and back*, so to speak, and there are very few forms of trendiness (no matter how bizarre or physically revolting) that they have not seen and treated before.

Dullwood is located on a flat, grassless plain near Hurley, South Dakota, about thirty-six miles from the thriving metropolis of Sioux Falls. As one approaches the center's imposing walls, the observer is struck by a conspicuous absence of sports cars, Lacoste shirts, and acupuncture clinics. One does not hear the thundering hooves of joggers and the painful wails of aerobic dancing. Phrases like "meaningful relationship," "I need my space," and "consciousness-raising" are unknown here. New-Agers and Trend-Setters do not stop at Hurley, South Dakota, except to get well, get dull, and get happy again.

If you or someone you love is suffering from the devastating effects of trendiness (weight loss, financial difficulties, ludicrous vocabulary, intolerance of friends, desire to inflict pain on oneself) consider *Dullwood*, the only generic solution to sound mental health.

A DULLWOOD CASE HISTORY

Lester J. Plenum was an unfortunate victim of imported mineral water, gold neckchains and singles bars. Luckily, loved ones took him to Dullwood . . .

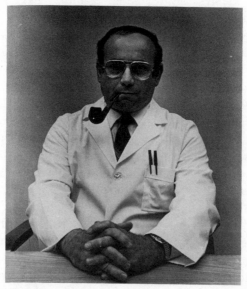

There, Dr. Ignatius B. Bland was waiting and ready . . .

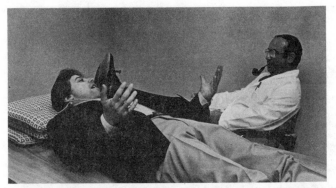

Without a moment to spare, doctor and patient began the lengthy consultation process ...

After careful analysis, Dr. Bland begins therapy, sensitizing Lester to the values of the Dull Lifestyle ...

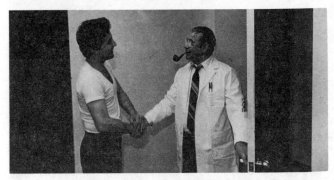

At last, after several grueling sessions, Dr. Bland congratulates Lester J. Plenum—now a proud Dullman. ANOTHER TRIUMPH FOR DULLWOOD!

Dull Yoga

The Dull Martial Arts: Prone-Fu

Consciousness-Raising Alternatives:

The list of items in the left-hand column represents a faddish and trendy consciousness. The list to the right represents their dull equivalents.

Instead of:	*Try:*
Wearing gold chains	Dog tags
Playing tennis	Ping-pong
Driving a Porsche or BMW	A Checker Marathon
Swapping wives	Swapping furniture
Diving for sunken treasure	Walking on the beach with a metal detector
Listening to Bruce Springsteen	Tony Bennett
Cocaine	Black coffee and a chew
Money magazine	*Consumer Reports*
Calvin Klein	J.C. Penney
Perrier	Salt-free seltzer
Vintage wine	A beer and a shot
Quiche	Pepperoni pizza
Collecting antiques	Collecting license plates
Marriage counseling	Boxing gloves
Aerobics	Wheezing
Holistic massage	A coin-operated vibrator bed
Backpacking	Reading the L.L. Bean catalog
Dabbling in the commodities market	Buying U.S. Savings Bonds
Sailing to Tahiti	Driving to Phoenix
A week in Switzerland	Two weeks in Switzerland

CHAPTER SEVEN

THE "NO-THRILLS" VACATION

Dulltours, Inc.

Dear Turnpike Adventurer,

At Dulltours, Inc., we believe our bus tours are an experience that will last a lifetime. For this reason, we will do everything possible to make your American or Canadian holidays safe and predictable. We live by the motto: ''This is your vacation. Why take chances?''

Our coast—to—coast network of recently repaired and repainted ''Lazyliner'' motorcoaches serve many cities with our dual—wheel comfort and diesel—engine hospitality.

And every single ''Lazyliner'' is *glass—bottomed* for your sightseeing pleasure!

With all this experience, we can make your journey seem much longer than it is, at no additional cost to you.

Bon Voyage,

Delbert P. Wince
General Manager
Dulltours Travel
and Aluminum Siding Company

The Dulltours Glass-Bottomed "Lazyliner"

Dulltour #1: Canadian Hideaway: The Golf Courses of MANITOBA!

7 long days and nights, from $799 per person

INCLUDES:
- Bus fare
- Complimentary lime Jell-O
- Deluxe Motel 6 Accommodations
- Free copy of *Canada: Young Giant of the North* (a $5.95 value)

OPTIONAL:
— Tour of the Union Stockyards, Winnipeg
— Visit to the Flin Flon Trout Festival (1st week in July only)

Tour Description

Thursday: We'll depart from Carroll, Iowa, on board the Lazyliner *Martin Van Buren*, by way of scenic Route 71, lunching at Iowa's highest point, the towering Ocheyedan Mound, 1,675 ft. Then it's on to Sleepy Eye, Minnesota, for a frank 'n beans dinner and a restful night's sleep on board your motorcoach.

Friday: Returning to scenic Route 71, we'll snack in Ottertail, Minnesota (try the ottertail) then proceed on up Route 59 all the way to beautiful downtown Winnipeg, where we'll spend a quiet evening practicing at our motel's private pitch 'n putt.

Saturday–Monday: It's golf, golf, golf, day and night, with a busy tour of the links in Winnipeg, Brandon, Carberry, Wasagaming, Gimli, and Pilot Mound. (We'll try to make it to Neepawa if we have time.)

Tuesday: After receiving our farewell *lei*, we'll depart Winnipeg on our way to North Dakota via gorgeous Route 29. Following lunch and a strafing demonstration at Grand Forks Air Force Base, we'll drive to Fargo on breathtaking Route 81 and make a quick visit to the West Fargo Industrial Park. Then it's an early supper at Howard Johnson's, and free time after that for you to visit local shops for crafts and souvenirs.

Wednesday: The last leg of our tour is a busy one, but well worth it. We'll visit Henry, South Dakota, and personally shake hands with all 182 inhabitants. After lunching on board just outside of Sioux Falls, it's just a short hop to Home Sweet Home via Le Mars, Correctionville, Early, and Sac City.

Dulltour #2: Sunbelt Serenade: A "Club Dead" Extravaganza for Dull Singles!

---

7 days, from $849 per person

INCLUDES:
- Bus fare, airfare, and all accommodations
- A 50-50 match of dull men and women
- Complimentary glass of Cold Duck
- Medical personnel on board
- Romantic flashlight dinners

Tour Description

This one-week fun-in-the-sun tour is a virtually non-stop romp through the sun belt's summer "hot spots." Since the whole idea is for you and your fellow passengers to "get acquainted" at your own leisurely and perhaps cautious pace, there's no pressure to actively participate in anything at all.

You don't even have to get off the bus if you don't want to.

We'll start off in beautiful Sun City, Arizona, and

meander aimlessly through New Mexico on our way to Club Dead's Caribbean Beach House in Corpus Christi, Texas.

After an exquisite Australian dinner and accordian serenade, it's off to bed (to sleep, of course) so we can get an early start on our Astrodome tour in Houston. Then it's a quick lunch at *Dos Gringos* and back on the road to Louisiana.

We'll carefully avoid New Orleans for a trip to Fort Polk where we will be the guests of the US Army Precision Truck Drill Team. There will be no time to waste as we head toward Pensacola and the Vernon Turkey Shoot.

After a quick look at the beautiful swamps around Tallahassee, we'll double back down the Gulf Coast to Disneyworld for two days of good clean fun.

Leaving our Lazyliner motorcoach in Florida, we'll hop on Club Dead's recently repaired and repainted DC-3 "Lovebomber" for a short flight to exotic Nuevo Laredo, Mexico, where you can wander around and enjoy the "old world" atmosphere, perhaps play a little co-ed water polo in the Rio Grande, or just sit in the town square and watch the ingenious mechanics weld buses back together.

On day six, a Club Dead Lazyliner will meet you once again for the more leisurely last leg of your Sun Belt Serenade. This is the best time to get to know the name of the person sitting next to you, balance your checkbook, or perhaps begin to dream of your next turnpike adventure!

Dulltour #3: A Carefree Cultural Holiday: On Tour with the Broderick Crawford Dancers!

21 days, from $1299 per person

INCLUDES:
- Bus fare and all Motel 6 accommodations
- Complimentary Toast (white or rye)
- Preferred seating at all performances

Tour Description

Here's an opportunity to mingle on a day-to-day basis with a troupe of unusual artists who have been startling audiences all over the country. The Broderick Crawford Dancers are dedicated to reaching out to "real" audiences in the "real" world. Eschewing trendiness and big-name talent, this Colorado-based group turns the mundane and the commonplace into an art form.

The B.C. Dancers Annual Tour will commence in Denver. Trailing their tour bus with the newly washed and tuned Dulltours Lazyliner *Millard J. Fillmore,* you'll live as they live and do as they do, in cities like Cheyenne, Laramie, Lincoln, Omaha, Des Moines, Fort Wayne, Toledo, Dayton, Paducah, Little Rock, Tulsa, Wichita Falls, Albuquerque, and Colorado Springs.

Under the direction of choreographer Leif "Elvis" Steinert, the troupe will perform their entire repertoire, in spite of the recent defection of three lead dancers to the Soviet Union.

You will be an actual part of this dance-history-in-the-making. You will share their laughter, do their laundry and watch them stumble in this unforgettable whirlwind cultural adventure!

Dulltour #4: The Land of Thank You Please: A Grand Tour of London!

7 days, from $799 per person, October–March only

INCLUDES:
• Airfare and all accommodations
• Complimentary english muffin
• Full-time interpreter
• Miniature souvenir bust of George III

Tour Description

In response to numerous requests from previous Dulltours participants who wanted something "as exotic as Canada but a bit farther away," we've reconsidered our prejudice against foreign travel and created a wonderful Grand Tour of London, England.

You'll board your recently repaired and repainted Dulltours C-48 "Cloudfinder" aircraft at scenic Newark Airport late Saturday night for the restful sixteen-hour flight to Heathrow Airport.

Upon arrival, you will be wisked aboard a freshly tuned and serviced London Transport bus to your quaint basement rooms at the Hilton, where you'll find a familiar "at-home" feeling and attractive off-season rates.

On Monday, we'll be off very early, for a quick on-foot journey to Marble Arch, where we'll embark on an exciting rush-hour 'Round London Sightseeing Tour. Picking our way leisurely through traffic, we'll view over twenty miles of famous London landmarks, including St. Paul's, Westminster Abbey, and the Reject China Shop on Beauchamp Place. If time permits, we'll catch the Richard M. Nixon exhibit at Madame Tussaud's Wax Museum and the Crown Jewels of the World exhibit at Westminster (don't worry, they're all fake!).

As evening falls, we'll head back to our hotel for an all-American dinner and a look at everyone's childrens' wedding pictures.

Tuesday will find us speeding merrily down to Croydon for a shopping spree at the Whitgift Centre pedestrian precinct. You'll have the entire day to look for local crafts and perhaps tour the famous Whitgift Almshouses.

For the more adventurous, there's the opportunity to go a bit further afield and take in the Wimbledon Lawn Tennis Museum and the Chessington Zoo, which contains the world's largest collection of sleeping animals. Please be assured that at all tour stops the water is perfectly safe for drinking.

From Wednesday to the following Saturday we will pursue a more detailed tour of London proper, with an emphasis on participating in local traditions and customs, such as trying out the famous echo chamber in the British Museum reading room.

Evenings will be spent in various cultural pursuits for which London is so famous, including the "British Coal Mining in Art" exhibit at the Science Museum and, of course, Brahms' German Requiem at Barbican Hall.

On Sunday morning we will reluctantly conclude our English holiday with a farewell spam-and-eggs breakfast in this ageless City of Magic. Turning our props westward, we will swiftly journey home, comforted in the knowledge that our camera bags are filled with countless snapshots and our memories brimming over with somewhat indescribable experiences.

P.S. Some handy tips for the London visitor:
1. All brothels are clearly marked with blue lights.
2. Your hotel chambermaid will greatly appreciate you hanging your mattress out of the window in the morning.

Review Exercises for Chapter Seven

1. Make a list of at least six awful things that could happen to you in a foreign country. Remember that Alaska and Hawaii are part of the U.S., so don't list frostbite and pineapple wounds.

_____

_____

_____

_____

_____

_____

Answers: There are many correct answers to this question. If you have listed just *two* of the following, give yourself 100%. If you've listed *one,* give yourself 65%: being hijacked; having your passport eaten by communist ducks; being trapped at a Club Med let's-get-naked party; selling your pants to a KGB agent; running over a Sicilian's chickens; accidently ordering a meal in London; being forced to yodel in public; going to a restaurant and being served something that still has the head on it.

CHAPTER EIGHT

DULL CULTURE, *HAUT ET BAS*

This Week At the Dulldome

At Cinema Zero
(Mon.–Thurs.)

The Film Cans Festival
A most unusual exhibit on the style and use of film cans throughout the world, including a rarely seen Czechoslovakian specimen made from a pair of hinged Skoda hubcaps.

(Fri.–Sun.)

A Lassie Retrospective

At the Museum of the Ordinary
(Mon.–Sun.)

The John Glenn Exhibition Hall is featuring our exciting *Vegetables of Emerging Nations*. Of special interest is the *manioc*, a tasteless tuber which is often used as a base for airline food.

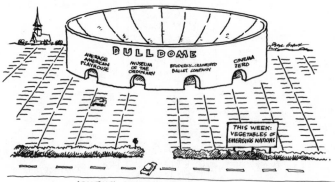

DULLDOME
IN CARROLL, IOWA
(UNINFLATED)

ARCHITECT'S RENDERING OF THE DULLDOME CULTURAL COMPLEX
(ESTIMATED COMPLETION DATE: JANUARY 16, 1985)

At the Broderick
Crawford Ballet
Theater
(Mon.–Fri.)

The U.S. premiere of *Spartacus vs. the Highway Patrol.*

(Sat.–Sun.)

The B.C. Ballet's own special version of the *Nutcracker Suite* will be performed each and every weekend for the entire ballet season. Using the clever device of strapping cinder blocks on the dancers' feet, thousands of walnuts are actually crushed on stage during the performance. Don't miss this unusual, though not necessarily quiet, dance spectacular!

At the Average
American Playhouse
(Mon.–Sun.)

The Shakespearian Tragedy Dinner Theater will present four alternating tragedies with a different corresponding menu each week during the theater season. This week's selection will be *Macbeth* with bar-b-que spare ribs, home fries and a choice of beverage. (Kitchen closes immediately after the banquet scene.)

In the Lobby
(Exhibits change periodically. Check the Schedule of Events Calendar.)

History of the fork; greatest speeches of Dwight David Eisenhower; snacks and their origins; from ancient fish stick

to modern french fry; pillow-
cases from the fifty states; thirty
years of motel ashtrays; Monto-
vanni, McKuen, and Manilow:
their lives, their work, their favorite recipes.

A Dull Man's Guide to The Arts

Far from being artistically impoverished, the dull man
takes every opportunity to enjoy the arts, and is fully
prepared to be dragged by his date, wife or friends
to a cultural experience. With the proper attitude and the
ability to be selective, an appreciation of The Arts can be
relatively painless and reassuringly uneventful.

Ballet

Ballet was invented one afternoon by Louis XIV about
four hundred years ago. Looking for something to do (not
uncommon among kings), Louis decided to dress up some
peasants in panty hose and silly costumes and make them
act like puppets in time to music for the amusement of
the culturally deprived. This quaint feudal custom is still
very popular today.

The cultured Dull Man arrives at the theater with a
good meal and a few stiff drinks under his belt, and buys
the cheapest seats in the last row of the highest balcony.
A long, dark ballet is preferable (Tchaikovsky is recommended) to allow the dull patron of the arts to be asleep
as soon after the opening curtain as possible.

Intermission is an excellent opportunity for two more
Manhattans, a trip to the men's room, and a good cigar.
At the resumption of the ballet, the delightful snooze is
begun again, to be rudely interrupted at the final curtain

by obligatory thunderous applause. It is impolite to leave before everybody stops clapping.

Opera

The discerning Dull Man prefers German operas no shorter than six hours, with the usual complement of at least 120 singers and one dozen barnyard animals. *Die Meistersinger von Nürnberg* is highly recommended. Avoid trendy modern operas and any singer who is a current media darling, or has recorded songs in English.

Art

The safest place for the cultivated Dull Man to view "art" is either in a museum or an art gallery. The French Impressionists in the National Gallery in Washington D.C. are reliably unexciting, and having a few glasses of wine in the basement of the Whitney Museum in New York while appreciating Andy Warhol could make a hummingbird doze off in midflight.

The key word around art museums or galleries is "interesting." Whenever you are rudely awakened, just mutter "interesting."

Drama

The dull lover of the thespian arts must be very careful in choosing suitable theatrical entertainment, since the very object of drama is to excite the audience. This can be avoided by attending Beckett revivals. If these are not readily available, try Shaw or Chekhov done by local theater groups. Shakespeare can be a bit risky for the dull theatergoer, but if all the actors start screaming in the first act, you know you're O.K.

If you are unsure about when a film is a "movie" and when it is "cinema," just remember this simple rule: If it makes lots of money, it's a *movie*. If you study it in college, it's *cinema*.

Film makers have long recognized the tremendous market in catering to the needs of the dull audience. In the past few years, the dull moviegoer has been especially fortunate, with the advent of the phenomena known as the *sequel* and the *sequel*-to-the-*sequel*.

No guide to the cinema would be complete without a preview of a few of these predictable sequels-to-come:

ROCKY XVII

After the heavyweight crown falls to an avowed homosexual from San Francisco named the *Castro Kid*, Rocky Balboa is called out of retirement at age seventy-two to fight once again. Billed as the "Great Straight Hope," Rocky plans to defeat his younger opponent by feigning death just before the opening bell. We can't tell you the cliché-ridden ending, but Sylvester Stallone has *plenty* of speaking parts, so bring a pillow and a meatball hero.

E.T., MBA

After returning to earth on a cattle-mutilating expedition (*The Return of E.T.*), and an unsuccessful marriage to Shelley Winters (*The Courage of E.T.*), our favorite extra-terrestrial overcomes his problems with child abuse (*E.T. Dearest*) and is accorded special minority status by the state of California. Using his grant money to further his education, E.T. attends the Harvard Business School and graduates in two days, whereupon he accepts a job with IBM (contingent on his continuing speech therapy) and moves to Atlanta. This is a film you will see over and over again, whether you want to or not.

THE EMPIRE RINGS YOUR DOORBELL AND RUNS AWAY
In this eighth segment of the *Star Wars* octology, an aging Darth Vader moves with his wife Ella to a suburb of Minneapolis. Resigned in his failure to conquer the universe, Darth begins to enjoy his new role as a model citizen, and eventually is elected to the local library board. His idyllic life is shattered, however, by a vicious band of Halloween thugs who soap the windows of his Dodge station wagon. With the blind fury of a wounded beast, Darth seeks revenge upon his neighbors, Han and Debbie Solo. T-shirts on sale now!

LE CHAT EST MALADE
(In French, with French subtitles.) This twenty-sixth addition to director Eric Rohmer's series of moral tales tells the intriguing story of a frail young woman who, without apparent motivation, falls in love with a saxophone and then spends the rest of her life talking about it. Hailed by the European press as "a grinding bore," *Le Chat Est Malade* has already won three American film festival awards on the basis of some outtakes stolen from the editor's trash can. The thirty-four minute "face-in-the-puddle" scene is not to be missed.

The Delbert Awards

Dull films have been around as long as films have been made; yet the misguided and trendy within the motion-picture industry refuse to grant these cinematic gems the critical acclaim they so richly deserve. "Oscars" are given to films or individuals who purport to exhibit a consistent and recognizable talent; however, the critics have failed to realize that it takes a certain genius to make a film *totally* dull, unexciting and predictable. *Anybody* with lots of money can make a film that people will talk about, but what about those studios, those directors, producers, and actors who have made absolutely *unmemorable* films, ones that can be viewed time and time again in undisturbed tranquillity. Dull audiences *love* dull movies, and it's time they were given some respect.

It is in keeping with these ideals that the Delbert Awards were created and bestowed. The Delbert Awards were first presented in 1980, in honor of Delbert Plank, a budding dull film maker who enrolled at UCLA in the late 1970s, determined to "do something on film that had never been done before." Within weeks, his brilliantly sedate and uninspired Super-8 classic *My Pal, Claudius* appeared, using voice-overs and a cast made up entirely of gerbils. Plank's lackluster career was brutally terminated when, during an outing with fellow film students, he fell or was pushed into a pit of Los Angeles lawyers who were behind in their car payments. Death did not come quickly.

Unlike the Oscars, the Delberts can be given *and* taken away every year, so that consistently dull artists might be rewarded time and time again while trendy imposters can be punished for backsliding.

May I have the envelope, please?

CATEGORY: Dullest Studio/ English language/ Animation or Live Action
Walt Disney Studios
In animation—everything since *Dumbo*
In live action—everything

CATEGORY: Dullest Producer
David Begelman
for *Buddy Buddy, Brainstorm, Pennies from Heaven, Rich and Famous* and *Yes, Giorgio.*

CATEGORY: Dullest Director/ Foreign Language:

Ingmar Bergman (Sweden)
> Hands down, no contest.

CATEGORY: Dullest Cinematic Series/ Foreign Language:
Tora-San (Japan)
> Twenty-Three (yes, count 'em) films about the adventures of a dull guy in a pork-pie hat.

CATEGORY: Dullest Actress
A three-way tie between
Candice Bergen
Ali McGraw
Brooke Shields

CATEGORY: Dullest Actor
A three-way tie between
Peter Fonda
George Segal
Alan Alda

CATEGORY: Dullest Supporting Actor
Burt Young

CATEGORY: Dullest Supporting Actress
Ruth Gordon

CATEGORY: Dullest Sports Film
Dreaming—
> The story of a young bowler who tries to break into the pro circuit.

CATEGORY: Dullest Drama (maybe of all time)
Rich and Famous

CATEGORY: Dullest Western
A two-way tie between *Heaven's Gate* and *The Legend of The Lone Ranger*.

CATEGORY: Dullest Children's Film (ever)
            Chitty-Chitty Bang Bang

CATEGORY: Dullest Science-Fiction Film
            A two-way tie between *Black Hole* and
                3 Stooges in Orbit (no Curly, no fun!)

CATEGORY: Dullest Costume Drama (in the whole
            world, ever)
            Barry Lyndon

CATEGORY: Dullest 3-D Movie
            Treasure of the Four Crowns
            (It was so dull only two crowns were ever
                mentioned)

CATEGORY: Dullest Animal Film
            Benji

CATEGORY: Dullest Youth-Market Film
            R.P.M. (Anthony Quinn, Ann-Margaret)

CATEGORY: Dullest Political Documentary
            Any political documentary

CATEGORY: Dullest Gay Film
            Making Love (also winner of the prestigious
                Grand Bland Award)

CATEGORY: Dullest Motorcycle Movie (ever, most likely
            forever)
            C.C. & Company (Joe Namath, Ann-
                Margaret)

CATEGORY: Dullest Musical
            1776
NOTE: *Annie* was a close second, but we had to draw the
line between dull and *agonizing*.

CATEGORY: Dullest Shakespearian Adaptation
Othello, the Black Commando (Tony Curtis as Iago)

CATEGORY: The Dullest Remake
Lost Horizon (musical version)

CATEGORY: Dullest Independent Feature
Polyester (Divine and John Waters get respectable)

CATEGORY: Dullest Disaster Film/ made for TV movie
A two-way tie between
Smash-Up on Route 5 and *The Night the Bridge Fell Down* (Desi Arnez, Jr.)

━━━━━━━ Dull Man's Quiz #2 ━━━━━━━

Q. How can you spot a dull man at an art gallery?

A. He's the one admiring the thermostat.

65

CHAPTER NINE

DULL DIVERSIONS

You've probably heard the old saying: "All work and no play makes Jack a very dull boy." Unfortunately, while the axiom is good as far as it goes, work alone cannot bring a person to the blissful state of true dullness. Certain kinds of hobbies, as well as a good healthy dose of suitable diversions and distractions, are absolutely necessary to reinforce the dull state of mind when one is not at work.

This chapter is concerned with the best use of leisure time. What else is life about?

Suitable Hobbies and Pastimes for a Dull Man

Stamp or Coin Collection (also hubcaps, beer cans, books, string, toy trains, bits of aluminum foil)

Golf

Gardening (with emphasis on lawn care)

Bowling

Bingo

Building things (clothespins, popsicle sticks or toothpicks are acceptable building materials)

Calling up radio talk shows

Browsing (preferably at Sears)

Ping-Pong

Crossword puzzles (also Rubik's Cube, bridge, jigsaw puzzles, bar dice, matching coins)

Waxing a car

Painting by numbers

✗ Hosing off the front steps, sidewalk, or driveway

Alphabetizing record albums

Lawn darts

Watching airplanes take off

Reading the entire J.C. Whitney catalog at one sitting

Testing the garage-door opener

Playing chess by mail

Reading *Reader's Digest*

Dialing the time and temperature

Listening to a CB scanner

Checking out new models at the phone store

I would add Fishing in Nebraska

A Dull Man's Guide to Television

An appreciation of the medium of television is essential to a dull lifestyle. Not only does TV afford you the opportunity to never leave your house for entertainment, but it can, if used carefully, help you to become or remain the all-around dull guy you know and love.

The Dull and Correct Way to Watch Television

1. Equipment: A black-and-white TV is always duller than color, even though color TVs have those nifty remote devices that allow you to stay in your chair for days at a time. A possible solution to this dilemma is to adjust your color set for black and white. Your set should be neither too

large (overwhelming) nor too small (requires too much concentration). Cable TV is highly recommended, as are video recorders, provided that you use them to tape sports or yesterday's twenty-four-hour weather channel.

2. Schedules: By far, *TV Guide* is *the* recommended program guide. Referred to by some initiates as "the bible," it should always be within arms reach. Not only can you avoid surprises and plan ahead, but the articles in *TV Guide* are among the most noteworthy in dull literature.

3. Recommended Programs: Here are some suggestions to get you on the right track. After a few days of practice viewing, feel free to add similar shows of your own choosing.

CATEGORY	PROGRAM	DULLNESS RATING
News Show	MacNeil-Lehrer Report	Very good. Competent, humorless, nice even pace.
Mini-Series	*The Winds of War*	*TV Guide*'s description says it all: "Rhoda (Polly Bergen) drifts into an affair with Palmer (Peter Graves), and Natalie (Ali MacGraw)

		makes plans to marry Byron (Jan-Michael Vincent) in Portugal. Meanwhile, Hitler (Gunter Meisner) plots an invasion of the Soviet Union."
Soap Opera	*Romance Theater*	Excellent. Louis Jordan's sauveness adds a nice touch to the lives of common folk.
Talk Show	John Davidson	Very good. After all, he's Merv Griffin's replacement.
Cop Show	*Adam 12* reruns	Excellent. Dull cops fighting dull crime.
Comedy Series	Anything with McLean Stevenson	Wow! Did you catch *Condo* before it was canned?
Drama Series	*Quincy*	What can we say? It is, after all, about a coroner.
Western	*Father Murphy*	Superb. Foot-

I agree!

		ball players always make the best actors.
Animal Program	Lorne Greene's *New Wilderness*	Excellently dull. Just ask Ol' Mister Possum.
Annual Special	Anything with Bob Hope and the Dallas Cowboy Cheerleaders	Great. "But seriously folks . . ."
PBS Series (domestic)	Steve Allen's *Meeting of the Minds*	Inspirational. Formerly interesting actors rise above their talents.
PBS Series (foreign)	*Winston Churchill —The Wilderness Years*	Highly educational material for the dull. A detailed chronicle of that period in Mr. Churchill's life when he did absolutely nothing.
Public Service Announcements	Test of the Emergency Broadcast System	Excellent. Even duller than test patterns.
Late Night Comedy Series	*Fridays* or the entire 1981	Very amusing. A laugh-an-hour.

	season of *Saturday Night Live* (except for the night Bill Murray was host)	
Sports	*Celebrity Bowling* or The International Figure Skating Championship	Well worth your time, especially if you don't like annoying suspense.
Science Fiction Series	*The Invaders*	Top notch. Did you know that bad actors can't move their pinkies?
Religious Series	Sermonette	After a long day, there's nothing quite like a lesson in life drawn by an itinerant clergyman.
British Comedy	A four-way tie among Dave Allen, Benny Hill, and the Two Ronnies.	Excellent stuff here. A chance for Americans to see the other side of British television.
Cute Kid Show	Reruns of *Leave It to Beaver*	A legend in its own time.

Review Exercises for Chapter Nine

A Sports Quiz: Pick out your favorite moment in each of the following sports:

1. In football, I really enjoy:
    a) a ninety-yard run-back.
    b) when the winning quarterback takes the snap and falls down at the end of the game.
    c) the coin flip.

2. A baseball game wouldn't be the same without:
    a) a home run.
    b) an intentional base on balls.
    c) a rain delay.

3. The best part about watching golf on TV is when:
    a) there's a hole in one.
    b) a player marks his ball on the green with a coin.
    c) everybody starts looking for a lost ball.

4. Hockey is no fun without:
    a) a fight.
    b) watching a power play be killed off.
    c) watching the ice machine between periods.

5. In basketball, nothing can beat:
    a) dunking.
    b) time outs.
    c) stalls.

Dull Jogging

The dull jogger runs at night around his own block. He chooses practical garb, including a pair of 1963 Taiwanese tennis shoes, polyester shorts, a blue nylon windbreaker given to him by a major sparkplug manufacturer, and thin brown rayon executive hose with worn-out elastic. His style is shoulders pulled up to ears, elbows tight to sides, and stride choppy and flat-footed. Mentally, he is as poised as a neurotic hamster in a roll cage. As he doggedly explores the outer limits of his personal best, he looks forward to giving up in about two weeks.

· DULL JOGGING ·

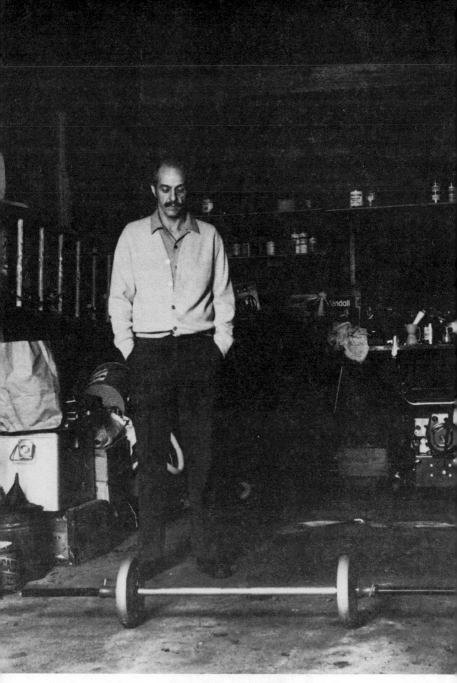

Dull Sports: Weightlooking

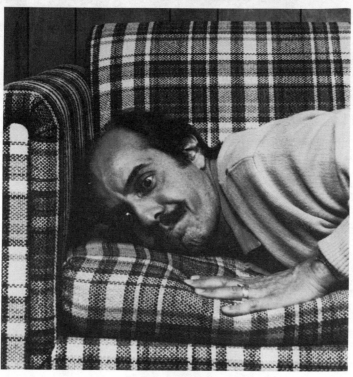

Dull Sports: Cheek-ups

Dull Sports: Hub Cap Frisbee

CHAPTER TEN

THE JOB OF COOKING

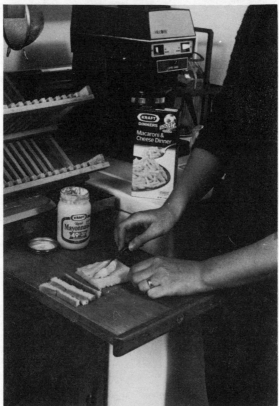

A Dull Woman performs two of the intricate steps toward preparing a Dull Meal

A Special Report From the President's Committee on Nutrition Among the Dull

In the summer of 1982, in Building Number Nine of the Andrew Stone Scientific Institute, located in Aspen, Colorado, a series of remarkable nutritional experiments were conducted on volunteer male laboratory mice. This groundbreaking inquiry into the effects of "dull" versus "trendy" eating habits (thereafter known in the scientific community as the A.S.S.I.–9 Report) has put forth significant new evidence to suggest that there is great truth to the old adage, "You are what you eat."

Although the actual procedures for these experiments are quite complicated and not easily understandable by laymen, the essential method used by the Institute was to feed two randomly selected groups of mice totally separate diets.

Group A, the *rodentia dullardia*, were given a "dull" diet consisting of foods like jellybean cake, mock apple pie made with ritz crackers, Mrs. Paul's Fishsticks (*lots* of Mrs. Paul's Fishsticks), twelve-egg omelettes from a local Greek restaurant, Tang, and olive loaf on white bread.

Group B, the *rodentia fashionablia*, were served small expensive portions of cheese-filled *croissant*, spinach salad, sole in lemon sauce, mineral water, chilled white wine, *paté de campagne* with wheat wafers, and broccoli quiche.

A control group, Group C, were fed a strictly macrobiotic diet, solely to punish them for not volunteering for Groups A or B.

Within one month of the implementation of this controlled diet plan, it was observed that Group A, when placed collectively on a balance beam scale opposite the collective Group B, weighed in at about twice the normal mass for mice of this breed; furthermore, Group A was spending as much as six hours per day watching afternoon television, while Group B spent an equal amount of time in group therapy. Within two months, the Group A mice had ceased any meaningful activity other than quietly puttering around the cage collecting things, tidying up, or laughing loudly in the corners with their buddies; on the other hand, Group B mice became frenetically active. This soon led to heavy drinking, drug abuse, and, inevitably, aerobics. Throughout these experiments, control Group C remained thin and sullen.

While it may be a bit premature at this time to declare the Stone Institute's findings incontrovertible, there is little doubt that one day it will be accepted as common knowledge that proper nutrition can play a major role in protecting the general public from the initially subtle but ultimately tragic effects of a trendy diet.

A Dull Man enjoys a home-cooked meal while reading his favorite magazine

The Job of Cooking: A Dull Woman's Guide to Menu Planning

Dull men are a lot like house pets. You put the same thing in their dish every day, and they're likely to hang around. Come to think of it, it's important to use the same dish, too. Dull guys don't like surprises, and in return for sturdy and reliable cuisine from your kitchen, you'll get their loyalty and admiration.

Here are some helpful hints (with our grateful thanks to the Industrial Food Institute of America) for feeding a Dull Man for an entire year. Just use the one week's worth of selections over and over again.

Atmosphere: Chrome dinette table with matching yellow vinyl chairs and placemats

or

Sears Roebuck dining table with wagon-wheel chairs

Plastic utensils, particularly knives and forks

Rectangular Styrofoam dinner plates, with compartments

Straw bowls with packets of Sweet 'n Low and saltines (as centerpiece)

Bunny rabbit salt-and-pepper shakers

Note: Whenever possible, serve all food directly from a microwave oven. The TV should be on at all times.

Breakfast: (should be the same every day)

A dish of plain oatmeal or Cheerios with powdered milk

Chris Glass of Tang or Hawaiian Punch

Instant coffee with nondairy creamer

Bowl of cottage cheese, no fruit

One underdone english muffin, Amtrak brand

Lunches: (you may vary these each day)
Deviled ham salad with crumbled potato chips
Bologna sandwich (optional: olive loaf)
Peanut butter on white bread

Tom
caven   Spaghetti-Os, preferably as a sandwich
Cup-O-Soup (optional: Cup-O-Noodles)
Baked beans on toast (dull Englishmen only)
Iceberg lettuce salad with ketchup and mayonnaise dressing; Velveeta cheese squares may be added

Quik-'N-Easy Dinners:
Frozen chicken pot pie
Minute steak with instant mashed potatoes and frozen peas
Liver ribbons with canned succotash
Macaroni-and-cheese casserole
Frozen pizza
Tuna melt with potato chips
Meat Loaf with canned baby potatoes and lima beans

Tasty Desserts:
Instant tapioca or butterscotch pudding
Lime Jell-O mold with canned fruit cocktail
Rice Krispy squares with Kool Whip topping
Toasted pound cake with plain vanilla ice cream
Reese's Peanut Butter Cups with a can of root beer
Any pastry purchased from a vending machine

The Dull Kitchen

═══ Dull Man's Quiz #3 ═══

Q. How can you recognize a dull man at a wine-tasting?

A. He's the one who asks to smell the twist-off cap.

CHAPTER ELEVEN

HIRING THE DULL

The Dull Businessman on the Go

Recommended Occupations for Dull People

Not everyone can have an exciting job, and it's a good thing that they don't. Without the millions of dull workers plugging away day after day, the country would collapse into ruin. The dull, being intensely loyal (from inertia) and virtually immune to boredom (by nature) are model employees, often shamefully unappreciated, brutally up-staged and pushed aside, *and yet totally indispensible.*

The dull do not harass employers with demands for "meaningful life-work;" they ask instead for a TV set at their work station. They do not sit and ponder the color of their parachute; rather, they go down with the ship.

Here is but a partial list of actual jobs held by gradu-ates of the *Famous School for Dull Men.* Use it as a guideline for choosing a career that is best suited to your own particular style of dullness. Most of all, be proud, dull person, in your work. Remember our battle cry: *"The Dull Get the Job Done!"*

Accountant/bookkeeper
Lawyer (corporate or tax)
Dentist
Postal or municipal employee
Banking (teller, loan officer)
Assembler (electronics, mechanical)
Computer programmer/data processor
Security guard (night shift)
Statistician (large company)
Insurance broker/claims adjuster
Bus driver (especially tours)
Proofreader
Sociology professor
Armed forces (noncombatant)
Inventory clerk
Toll collector
Projectionist
Vending machine/appliance repairman
Ticket-taker
Supermarket checkout clerk
Librarian
Administrator (education)
Manager (fast-food chain or department store)
Volkswagon mechanic
Meter reader
Gas-station attendant (night shift)
Baggage handler
Editor (trade journals)
Short-order cook
Telephone-company employee
Parking-lot attendant
Doorman
Stockbroker (large company, branch office)
Industrial film maker
Photo lab technician
Research assistant (obscure, under-funded project)
High school English teacher (after three years)

Counter (traffic, fish, people, anything)
Salesman (especially everyday items, like shoes and tires)
Car salesman (especially at a Chrysler or AMC dealership)

━━━━━━━━ Dull Man's Quiz #4 ━━━━━━━━

Q. How can you identify the dullest man among your fellow
employees?

A. He's the one with the sign that says "Thank God It's
Monday."

APPENDIX A

FINAL GRADING

Final Grading

In order to be awarded the title "Certified Dull Person" (which will allow you to use the initials C.D.P. after your name) you must total up all your scores at the end of each chapter in the following manner:

1. List your grade for each chapter:
   Ch. 3 _____
   Ch. 4 _____
   Ch. 5 _____
   Ch. 7 _____
   Ch. 8 _____
   Ch. 9 _____
   Ch. 10 _____
2. Then, throw out the scores of any *two* chapters you did poorly in.
3. Now add up the remaining six scores and put the total here: _____
4. Take this total from step 3 above, and divide by your age, rounding upward to the nearest whole number. Put this total here: _____
5. Then multiply the total in step 4 by your zip code and indicate here: _____
6. If you have patiently followed all these directions and you're sitting there with this ridiculous number in front of you, you pass. Congratulations, and turn to the back cover for your Certificate.
7. If you didn't follow all these directions but you did score a passing grade in at least *four* chapters, you also pass. Good work. Now proceed to the back cover.
8. If you *didn't* follow directions and you *didn't* pass four chapters, you are either a) incurably trendy, or b) *beyond dull.* In either event, you are automatically banished to Los Angeles. We'll be over in the morning to make sure your place is empty.

INVENTIONS-IN-PROGRESS FOR DULL PEOPLE

Inventions-in-Progress for the Dull: Computerized Digital Display TV for Football or Soap Operas

Inventions-in-Progress for the Dull: The All-Season Hammock

Inventions-in-Progress for the Dull: Coin-Operated Dry Cleaning Booth (for those who wish to wear same clothes every day)

DULL MOMENTS IN HISTORY

334 B.C.	First recorded dull man in history, Philip Arrhidaeus of Macedonia, decides to stay home while his brother Alexander the Great goes off to conquer the world. "Conquer, smonquer . . . so what's in Persia anyway? The water's bad and they rob you blind."
March 15, 44 B.C.	Marcus Tedious, accountant to Julius Caesar, lectures the emperor on the importance of being exactly on time for meetings.
800 A.D.	Start of Dark Ages in Europe. The dull rejoice.
1200	Troublemakers in Italy start Renaissance in Dante's basement, initiating decline of Western civilization.
1542	Juan Rodriquez Cabrillo discovers San Diego, but doesn't tell anyone.
1577	Sir Francis Drake sails right past San Francisco Bay, failing to notice bridge.
1624	First settlers arrive in Albany, New York.
1642	Invention of the adding machine.
1816	Invention of the metronome.
1845	Mr. Aspdin, an Englishman, introduces Portland cement.
1846	Iowa attains statehood.
1860	Discovery of linoleum.
1876	Rutherford B. Hayes elected.
1884	Punch-card information processing invented by Herman Hollerith.

1889	John L. Sullivan defeats Jake Kilrain in 75 rounds.
1902	Michigan defeats Stanford in Rose Bowl, 49–0.
1922	*Reader's Digest* founded.
1952	President Truman designates September 17 as Citizenship Day.
1963	Tom Swift dies quietly in bed.
1964	Invention of the pop-top can.
1968	Lyndon Johnson lifts beagle by the ears; also shows world his appendix scar.
1976	*Statistics Canada* announces that 45 people in the Yukon speak Italian.
1976	Number of TV sets in Albania reaches new high of 4,500.
Jan. 16th, 1980	"National Nothing Day" officially recognized by a joint session of Congress after stirring address by the President of the Dull Men's Club. (See the *Rearword* of this book for details.)

REARWORD

THE FOLLOWING TEXT, TAKEN FROM ORIGINAL NOTES HANDWRITTEN ON THREE-HOLE LINED PAPER, IS A CONDENSATION OF A RECENT ADDRESS GIVEN BEFORE A JOINT SESSION OF THE CONGRESS OF THE UNITED STATES BY JOSEPH L. TROISE, FOUNDER AND PRESIDENT OF THE INTERNATIONAL DULL MEN'S CLUB.

Mr. President, distinguished members of Congress, my fellow Americans, Dull People of the World. I am speaking to you today in response to an insidious trend now weaving its way into the social fabric of our great country. I speak not of Communism, drugs in high school, or too many Japanese pickup trucks. Many of us are all too quick to point an accusing finger at such social issues, saying "There! There is the source of all our problems!"

In spite of all the theories brought forth by the sages of our time, couched in the most serious of economic or moral terms, *no one*—not Milton Friedman, not Nancy Reagan, not Bob Hope nor Billy Joel—has even once touched upon what I feel is at the very core of the Erosion of the American Way of Life. In a word, people are trying to be *too interesting*!

We, as a people, have grown too fast, too painfully. We are, in a word, *overaware*! The tragedy of overawareness strikes one out of two American homes, a statistic all the more alarming when one realizes that this rate of frequency exceeds visits from Jehovah's Witnesses. This disability is manifested by a compulsion to be in touch with everything, on top of everything, able to discuss everything, do everything, enjoy everything, pay attention to everything—in fact, actually *striving* to be "vital" and "vibrant"—"multifaceted," as the personal ads in the *Saturday Review* would say it. Surely, my good congresspersons, this compulsion must be arrested before it is too late, before all of us lose our marbles, so to speak. [*Polite applause.*]

What is the solution to this crisis, to the malaise of Overawareness that has turned a perfectly normal and reasonable People into a mob of hungry and wanton attention-getters? Shall the good and dull among us perish before this onslaught? Will all of us, along with our children and our children's children, lead a life of bean-sprouts rather than hamburgers, honey in our coffee rather than sugar, "relationships" rather than marriages, [*Dramatic pause*]—*MASSAGE INSTEAD OF SEX*? Will we, in fact, be forced to devote most of our waking hours, our productivity, our very lunchtime to the pursuit of trendiness? Ladies and Gentlemen, I think not! [*Mr. Troise attempts to pound rostrum for emphasis, but misses.*]

We as a People should not waste another minute of our precious time, resources and energy being hip! Never again should one of us fall prey to the illusion that life is something more than one big Dental Appointment; never again should one of us fork out two bucks for a glass of bubbly water with a lime in it, when deep down in our hearts we know it's really club soda made in a warehouse in Cleveland!

It's not an easy thing to ask a nation to suddenly change course, to become, as it were, a Dull People. Yet, it is undeniable that the Very Dull among us are our greatest strength. It is the dull, after all, who unlock the doors of this joint every morning. It is the dull who fix our cars, run our elevators, drive our cabs, type our reports, do our accounting, and brush the branches, so to speak, over the trail of our past deeds. They are the ones who really keep the country going. Behind every flashy facade sits a serious and fastidiously competent worker who keeps the whole damn ship afloat. Who do you think takes Mick Jagger's checks to the bank? One of those coke-fried sociopaths in fright wigs that you see jumping around on the tour bus? Not on your life! And what good are these smartass parachuting brain surgeons you run into at parties anyway? Are they the ones healing

98

lepers in Swaziland? And tell me, how many disdainfully superior intellectuals can tune up a Volkswagen? And who ever said that rafting in some icy river or crawling up the side of some godforsaken mountain was *fun?* It's not fun, it's *sick!*

[*Mr. Troise pauses, wipes his brow with a generic paper towel.*]

I have not stood here this half-hour to alarm this illustrious body, nor any of you either; rather, I bring a message of hope—hope that the unrecognized, the metabolically unenergetic, indeed the *dull of the earth* will become our next cultural heroes.

[*. . . At this point, Mr. Troise constructs an elaborate and brilliant synopsis of mankind's political, economic and spiritual history. The audience sits spellbound as he effortlessly weaves this complex historical tapestry into a powerful speculative scenario of the Future America and the ultimate emergence of the genetically superior, albeit devolved DULLMAN. With his clumsy yet powerful presence, and with his voice rising and falling rhapsodically, he plays the audience like a musical instrument. Soon they are poised on the edge of their seats, laughing, weeping, clutching their breasts.*]

. . . and shall not . . . nay, *will* not, perish from the face of the earth!

[*Conclusion of the address. Wild applause, floral accolades, laurel wreath offered, refused, offered again, refused again (this time more slowly), offered yet a third time, refused once more (with a pained expression). Utter pandemonium, desks and chairs uprooted, triumphant procession to front lawn of Capitol Building, where enormous bronze statue of William Bendix eating a hot dog is unveiled.*]

ABOUT THE AUTHOR

JOSEPH L. TROISE is a formerly interesting native of New York City who discovered the error of his ways and moved to a small town in Colorado. After attempting to marry the girl next door (who got wind of it and moved), Mr. Troise quickly ascended to the presidency of The International Dull Men's Club, which currently affords him many opportunities for bus travel.

VOTE FOR THE DULLEST PERSON OF THE YEAR

The International Dull Men's Club is holding a poll to decide 1983's dullest public figures. To cast your vote, just fill out the form below. Winners will be announced in early 1984.

1. *Anyone from Nebraska*
2. *especially Railroaders*
3. *& Railroad wives*
4. _____
5. _____
6. _____
7. _____
8. _____
9. _____
10. _____

Mail your entry before December 31, 1983 to:
Joseph L. Troise, President
The International Dull Men's Club
2111-M 30th Street, Suite 1117
Boulder, CO 80301